mini Messaging

The Art of Smart Texting

mini Messaging

The Art of Smart Texting

Ewha Womans University Press

mini Messaging

The Art of Smart Texting

by Jasper Kim

First published 31 March 2010
by Ewha Womans University Press
11-1 Daehyun-dong, Seodaemun-gu, Seoul, Korea 120-750
Tel.: 82-2-3277-2965, 2966 / 362-6076
Fax.: 82-2-312-4312
E-mail: press@ewha.ac.kr
Online Bookstore: www.ewhapress.com

Researched by Eunkyoung Choi
Designed by Hyejin Chung

Price: 7,000 won
ISBN 978-89-7300-869-8 13740

Printed in Korea

Make things as simple as possible, but not simpler.

—Albert Einstein

(mini) TABLE OF CONTENTS

THE SCIENCE OF SHORT MESSAGING STRATEGY (SMS): 20 RULES FOR THE 2.0 ENVIRONMENT

Introduction

WHY YOU NEED THIS BOOK ON MINI MESSAGING

Mini Messaging: The Art of Smart Texting relates to writing strategies primarily aimed for texting, microblogging, instant messaging (IM), smart phone messaging and other condensed digital communications. It is a modern day version of the classic writing textbook, Strunk and White's "Elements of Style" for the Web 2.0 environment, applied to digital messages with limited writing space such as Twitter, Facebook comments, smartphone messaging, and IM—collectively referred to as a "Mini Message"—packaged in a creative, succinct and user-friendly approach.

Mini Messaging is meant to be a fun yet informative short text relating to short texts. It is primarily aimed at Mini Messages, but it can also be applied to longer and more general writing styles. This "mini book" is packaged creatively to maximize its understanding potential and readership interest. But this mini book is not all play—underneath the creative packaging exists fundamental principles related to the "art" and "science" of using Plain English for short messaging strategies. Writing in Plain English—simple, concise sentences—has always been important, even before Web 2.0. But when you only have a few words to make your point using digital devices, then Plain English for the 2.0 environment—referred to as "Plain English 2.0"—becomes even more important.

Although books exist relating to texting marketing, etiquette and psychology, this is one of the first and only books related to Plain English 2.0 for new social media that provides related methods and strategies that employs minimal word usage. By taking this "mini word" approach, the book follows the same type of word constraints to those of the subject matter (Mini Messages). Given the enormous convergence towards new social media such as Twitter, Facebook and text messaging generally, this book will give you the necessary strategies to get maximum value out of all your Mini Messages.

WHY *MINI MESSAGING* IS IN A "MINI BOOK" FORMAT?

This book is short for a reason: less is more. This text could go on for hundreds of pages discussing various elements of writing in Plain English 2.0 for new social media. But the goal of this book is to provide the most effective techniques and tools for you to follow, and to provide them as quickly and as succinctly as possible. The reason for this is simple: if a text message or IM only gives you one or two sentences of writing space, then why shouldn't the writing rules for new social media also mirror our space-constrained 2.0 environment? The answer is it should. And that is why this book is written in a mini book format.

Ultimately, it is also easier to remember and incorporate strategies and rules that are shorter than longer. For this reason, the 40 rules of art and science for Plain English 2.0 in this book are each written in 1 to 2 sentences. Again, less is more.

By reading *Mini Messaging* and spending time thinking about these topics, you are likely to become a better and more strategic writer for the 2.0 environment.

TEXTSPACE: THE FINAL FRONTIER

What do Texters, Tweeters and Techies (which basically includes anyone using any mobile technology) all have in common?

They all need the ability to tell their story through Mini Messaging. In this Mini Messaging environment, every space, every letter, every number and even every emoticon must justify their existence. Else, they will be squeezed out. In other words, every textspace in this new "Mini Frontier" must "add value." Otherwise, it gets eliminated because there is simply not enough space for it. This is because the "Mini Frontier" can be as small as 140 characters.

Because textspace is now one of the scarcest resources, and one that can define you or your organization, it is now more important than ever to acquire the strategies essential to defining your Mini Message—albeit in Twitter, Facebook, blogs, emails or any other writing that exists within space constraints.

The next new frontier is the Mini Message—an ultra-shortened message (written or spoken) in any medium.

MINI MESSAGING FOR A MINI WORLD

We live in a mini world.

From mini computers to mini cars—everything has been miniaturized—converted to a distant relative that is shorter, smaller and more succinct.

I call this the 21st century's Mini Movement trend. We are all part of it.

TEXTUALIZE THIS!

We live in an era where time is short and demands are high. No matter what job you have or what school you're in, we all face the challenge of how to meet increasing demands in an era of increasingly less time and space. With each task we face, professional or personal, we communicate constantly.

As an everyday person using new technologies, we have increasingly less space than ever to convey our message. With Twitter, you only have 140 characters to make your point. With smartphones *and* Blackberries, you have just a few sentences to make your case. And with blogs and emails, you have just a few lines to a few sentences to express the same idea.

Welcome to the "brave new world" of Mini Messaging 2.0!

With any new era or technology, we can view it as a challenge or as an opportunity. Those who do not have a clear-eyed 2.0 strategic vision will be at a comparative disadvantage. But those who do have it will gain tremendous value. This is because you will now have arguably the most sought after skillset in the 21st century—the ability to condense and convey your Mini Message effectively. Analyze, or better yet, textualize this! Imagine negotiating, building a start-up, marketing or conducting diplomatic relations without a strategy. Sure it can be done. But those who have a game plan vis-a-vis a 2.0 strategy will ultimately be able do it most effectively.

GET SMARTER

Although you may not need a strategy for Mini Messaging your closest of friends, increasingly due to our wired and borderless world, the vast majority of your digital messages will be to people outside your inner circle. Whether it's using Twitter to go out the latest news, Facebook for the latest updates on friends or a brief Blackberry message. Whether professional, personal or somewhere in between. Sending "smart" Mini Messages will necessitate having a smart 2.0 strategy.

ENTER THE TECH TRIBE: TEXTERS 2.0

This rapidly growing group—Texters, Tweeters and Techies—collectively form what I call the 21st century's "Tech Tribe." We are all a member of the Tech Tribe, in one form or another, to one degree or another. If you use email, instant messaging (IM), mobile phones, Blackberry, iPhones, Skype, or any other digital communication medium, you are part of the Tech Tribe collective.

Being part of this Tech Tribe, we live in a 24/7 world of words. Technology has made us contactable almost anytime, anywhere. People originally thought that technology would lead to more extra time. But instead, it has led to more overtime. Working by sending a rapid fire series of Mini Messages not only during so-called "normal" business hours, but also late at night and on the weekend has become the "new normal." We are now sending Mini Messages at all hours—albeit at the office, on the road, at home or even on the beach—due to the 2.0 environment.

BE THE "MASTER OF YOUR MINI MESSAGE"

An expression in law exists that the person making a contract offer is the "master of his offer." This means that the person making the offer has the advantage of being able to set the exact tone and terms of the offer made. Similarly, by writing any Mini Message—in Twitter, Facebook or anywhere else—you (rather than others) have the opportunity to be the "Master of your Mini Message."

Much like the expression, "you never have a second chance to make a first impression," you also rarely have a second chance to make a first impression in your Mini Message. Once you click the "send" button, your Mini Message is forever digitally memorialized.

YOU ARE YOUR MINI MESSAGE

Think about it this way: is it not in your best interest to figure out how to create "smart value" by choosing highly calibrated language that can elicit exactly the types of responses, imaging and emotions you want? Is it not in you or your organization's best interests to know how to most effectively minimize the likelihood of damage (in a defensive way) by avoiding critical mistakes that are virtually impossible to retract? I'm sure the answer to both is a resounding "yes!"

What is the benefit of converting simple "write as you think" words to a Mini Messaging strategy? It will give you a competitive advantage in conveying your version of the story in the most clear, convincing and concise way possible.

THE SHORT MESSAGING STRATEGY (SMS)

Because we all live in a 24/7 Mini Messaging environment, then the issue becomes how to turn this change into an opportunity.

How do we do this? By having an effective means to transform any short message to Mini Messages—Tweets, texts, blogs, IMs, emails and so forth—into structured strategic and catchy digital sound bites.

This is your "Short Messaging Strategy" (SMS).

MINI MESSAGING: THE ART AND SCIENCE

One of the most cited books in war and business is Sun Tzu's *The Art of War*. It is popular because it gives strategy on outmaneuvering one's opponents, depicted as if it was an art form. Similarly, this book provides the "art" and "science" behind Mini Messaging and Short Messaging Strategy (your "SMS"). The "art" of SMS comes in the form of how to package your Mini Message—think of it broadly as the Mini Message's "style." The "science" of SMS comes in the form of easy-to-remember and applicable grammatical suggestions for writing your Mini

Message—think of it broadly as the Mini Message's "substance." Both are tailored specifically for the Mini Messaging "don't waste even one space" environment.

In the same spirit of Sun Tzu's *Art of War*, *Mini Messaging*: *The Art of Smart Texting* is useful for many purposes. On the "defensive" side, all of us have had our fair share of texting travesties. It just takes one misstatement, misspelling, or misinterpretation to lose a friend, acquaintance, opportunity or client. On the "offensive" side, having an effective Mini Messaging strategy will give you a competitive advantage of getting maximum impact from each of your Mini Messages in whatever form.

MINI MESSAGING FOR A 2.0 ENVIRONMENT

For each of this book's 2 main sections—the Art and the Science—the 20 most applicable strategies for maximizing the clarity, value and persuasiveness of your Mini Message is given to you.

This book will also be written in a way that reflects the Mini Messaging writing domain—short simple strategies, each written in less than one page—to mirror the Mini Messaging 2.0 environment in substance and style.

STRATEGY EQUALS SUCCESS

In short, *Mini Messaging* gives you the strategies necessary to convert a plain neutrally worded and unstructured sentence or message into a highly calibrated Mini Message.

May these strategies help you with all your future Mini Messages!

THE "ART" OF SMS: 20 RULES FOR THE 2.0 ENVIRONMENT

RULE

1

KEEP IT SIMPLE AND SPEEDY (KISS 2.0)

Your Mini Message should be concise and less than 1 page screen. To accomplish this, your Mini Messaging strategy is to "Keep It Simple and Speedy" (KISS 2.0). The old rule was Keep it Simple and Short. But in our Tech Tribe era dominated by Twitter, i-reporting and constant internet access, our 24/7 interconnected wireless Mini World of Mini Messages, time is constantly of the essence. And we are always seeking more things in less time that is driven by the need for hyper speed. So hit the ground running. And avoid the need for the "page down" button.

eXAMPLE (PRE-SMS)

Thank you for the email you sent me yesterday. Regarding your message, I will revert back to you after checking with my colleagues.

eXAMPLE (POST-SMS)

Thanks, and will revert back after checking with my colleagues.

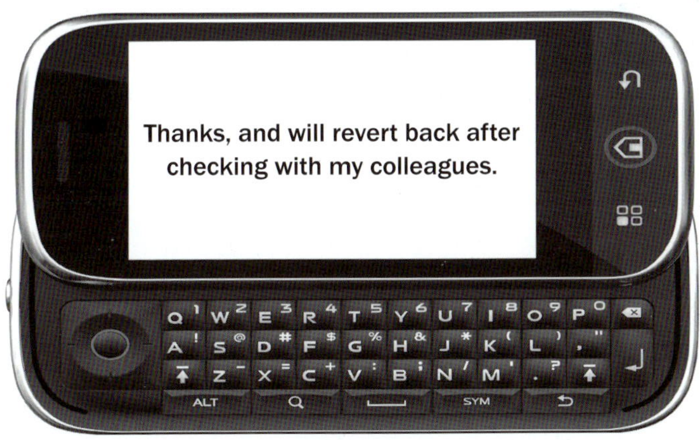

EXCEPTION

When dealing with your client or counterpart for the first time or when writing the initial message, KISS 2.0 can be applied more flexibly. This is because initial contact sets up the context for future Mini Messaging.

eXAMPLE

Hi, I'm Siouxie. I'll be handling your account. And I will be sending you a follow-up email later with our prices.

RULE 2

TRY TO BE PC (PUNCTUAL AND CLEAR)

"Being PC" used to mean being politically correct. But now in the 21st century's Mini Movement, being PC instead means being "punctual and clear." This is because the concept of time has shifted dramatically. Waiting 24 hours today for a reply can seem like an eternity. So your Mini Message should be returned within several hours, not several days. When replying, be extremely clear by focusing on one specific point.

eXAMPLE (PRE-SMS)

Appreciate your thoughts on our sponsored concert. Venue is Metropolitan Hall. Times will vary depending on the day. Weekday concerts are usually 7pm and weekend events are 6pm and 8pm, twice per day at night. Doors will open no earlier than 30 minutes before the concert begins.

eXAMPLE (POST-SMS)

Appreciate your thoughts on our concert. Venue is Metropolitan Hall. Other specifics will follow soon via email.

EXCEPTION

When a request for information is not directly being made, then you have the option of either leaving the Mini Message "as is" (i.e., no reply until further notice) or replying via a simple acknowledgement that you received the Mini Message.

eXAMPLE

Really enjoyed your last Facebook comment. Hope to see more soon.

RULE 3

COLLOQUIAL CONNECTION

Being "colloquial" means communicating through "ordinary or familiar conversation." This is now more important than ever. Write in simple prose. This is because you want to have the largest audience possible. And by using colloquial language, you form a "colloquial connection." Else, you risk a colloquial disconnect.

eXAMPLE (PRE-SMS)

Maximizing the number of attendees for our next event is critical for our long-run corporate objective. With respect to this matter, we require all personnel's immediate input and active participation.

eXAMPLE (POST-SMS)

Our goal is to get as many people out to our next event as possible. To make this happen, we would really appreciate all of your help and support.

EXCEPTION

States (government workers, bureaucrats, those not from the U.S.), seniors (either senior level personnel or the elderly) and so-called experts (consultants, academics) may prefer more formalistic language because this often mirrors their specific environment.

eXAMPLE

Dear Distinguished Dr. Noh, it was a true pleasure meeting you at last evening's dinner. I hope to keep in close touch going forward.

RULE 4

GET IN, GET OUT (GIGO)

Before writing anything, define your Mini Message's exact "mission" (objective). Then work backwards (reverse engineer) to decide what words will most effectively accomplish the Mini Message's mission. Get to your point, then get out immediately. I call this your GIGO ("Get In and Get Out") standard. If you use GIGO, you have a standard by which to filter words. Afterwards your Mini Message will effectively represent a precise laser—guided missile in verbal form. Without GIGO, your Mini Message may veer dramatically off course, jeopardizing the Mini Message's mission.

eXAMPLE (PRE-SMS)

There's an upcoming event that we would like to tell you all about. The event is an open-to-all signing party. The day of this signing part will be this Friday at 7pm. Again, everyone is invited to this event.

eXAMPLE (POST-SMS)

Signing party this Friday 7pm. Everyone's welcome. See you all there!

EXCEPTION

If you want to have your Mini Message crescendo (build up) into a climactic conclusion, then you can forego GIGO.

eXAMPLE

Guess what's happening this Friday at 7pm?! It's the moment you've all been waiting for—that's right—it's the big signing event open to all. Hope to see you all there!

RULE

5 FRAME (ISSUE) FIRST

A star Hollywood director sees his/her movie one frame at a time through the perspective of the director's camera lens. The reason is that some scenes look different outside the frame than inside. You are the director and your Mini Message is one film frame. So, as the "Master of your Mini Message," decide how you want to frame your message. Often this is done by isolating a specific "issue."

eXAMPLE (PRE-SMS)

One of the agenda items I'd like to follow-up on is how to pass our next budget. To do this, we ideally need to have a five percent tax credit for certain members of the committee. What do you think?

eXAMPLE (POST-SMS)

Hi Monica. Central issue is how to pass the budget with a 5% tax credit—agreed?

EXCEPTION

For events that are more social than business oriented, then the "Frame First" approach may seem slightly rigid and less approachable.

eXAMPLE

Come one, come all—an alumni meet-and-greet session next Tuesday—come as you are.

RULE 6

FIRST IN, LAST OUT (FILO)

We all know the adage "you never have a second chance to make a first impression." Translated for the Tech Tribe world, your Mini Message's first sentence often represents its first impression. In other words, your first sentence leaves a lasting impression. I call this the First In, Last Out (FILO) effect. So, based on the FILO effect, make your Mini Message's first sentence memorable. In other words, make it a "deep impact" sentence. This can be done by making it short, dramatic, controversial or in question form.

eXAMPLE (PRE-SMS)

Shoes are important for everyone. The great thing about our newest line of running shoes is that they are environmentally-friendly in the sense that they are biodegradable.

eXAMPLE (POST-SMS)

Save the earth, buy our biodegradable shoes!!

EXCEPTION

If you are Mini Messaging in "defensive" mode (to remedy a complaint or explain a sensitive issue), then you can pay less attention to the FILO effect.

eXAMPLE

Dear Mr. and Mrs. Smith, we appreciate your business and have been informed about your concerns. We will look into this matter immediately. Meanwhile, we're hopeful you will continue to be an invaluable customer for us.

RULE 7

AUDIENCE AWARENESS

In the 1990s, some movie theaters would run a sound test that displayed the wide range of their audio system. This was followed by a simple screen message: “the audience is listening.” Similarly, think of how your audience may be “listening” to your Mini Message. I call this your “Audience Awareness” ability. Ultimately, the “audience” (other texters, tweeters, etc.) usually seek clarity and quality. So, write more from your audience’s perspective than your own.

eXAMPLE (PRE-SMS)

We at Princely Paisley Pub pride ourselves on providing a fun and exciting environment for the last 17 years. One of our fine traditions is our famed Happy Hours, which are on weekdays from 5 to 7pm. Hope you can join us in this lively tradition.

eXAMPLE (POST-SMS)

Want to party like it's 1999? Then join us at the Princely Paisley Pub's Happy Hour. Every weekday from 5 to 7pm.

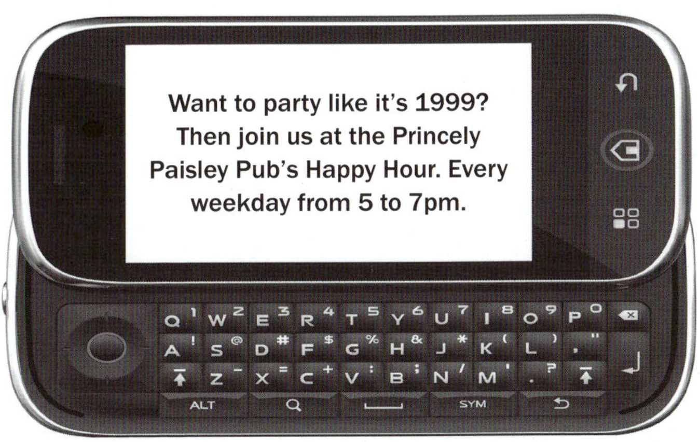

EXCEPTION

"Internal" messages to colleagues or other "insiders" may not always require an Audience Awareness ability. This is because "insiders" by definition or circumstance will already be in sync with the perspective from which you're messaging.

eXAMPLE

What's going on with Jane in PR, did you see her last email?

** Note*

PR=Public Relations department

RULE

8

DR. FILL SYNDROME

People generally have a tendency to use all the space allotted to them. This goes for writing (think, 20 page final reports) as well as other things as mundane as packing a suitcase for a trip. Studies have proven this. I call this temptation to fill the screen to the max with often unnecessary words as the "Dr. Fill" syndrome. Remember, in today's environment,"less is more." Just by virtue of knowing the "Dr. Fill" syndrome will allow you to better edit yourself. One way of accomplishing this is to confirm that every word "adds value."

eXAMPLE (PRE-SMS)

Hi Guys. I'm having a get together at my place this Saturday. It's going to be potluck style. Jai, can you bring drinks? Sonya, can you bring chips n' salsa? Jean, can you bring dessert? Thanks a bunch! Johnny (Max Word Count capacity filled)

eXAMPLE (POST-SMS)

Potluck at my place Saturday! Jai-drinks, Sonya-chips & salsa, Jean-dessert? Til then! Johnny

EXCEPTION

Certain "old school" bosses and other types may hold on to the notion that forgoing space is forgoing an opportunity to say more. If you're in this situation, fill more but still make sure every word "adds value."

eXAMPLE

Dear Mr. David Gone. We have not yet received your last response to our "Best of the 80s Bands" survey. As an icon of this music genre, your response is critical for us. Thus, we look forward to your reply shortly—Bill Bored Magazine Staff

RULE

9 EMOTICON ETIQUETTE

Don't get emotionally attached to your emoticons. They should be used sparingly for instances in which you've built a personable rapport where using emoticons will further, not fracture, the relationship.

eXAMPLE (PRE-SMS)

Thanks for the invite!:) I'd definitely LOVE to go ^.~ And can't wait for the buffet dinner ^@^ Too bad it's so expensive though :(:(

eXAMPLE (POST-SMS)

Thanks for the invite! And can't wait for the buffet, just hope it's worth the price :)

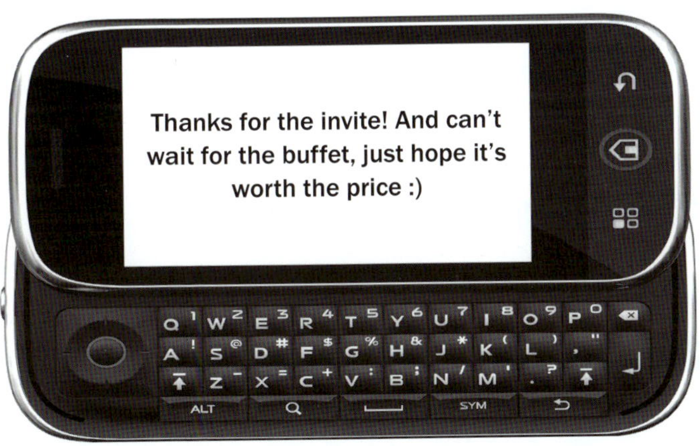

EXCEPTION

When dealing with "insiders" (close friends, family, etc) who are familiar with and enjoy using emoticons, then emoticons can be used more frequently, but not excessively.

eXAMPLE

Mom, Dad, Sis (^.^) Can't wait to see ya'll at the Ranch this Christmas!!)^@^(

RULE 10

DOSE OF DRAMA

If your Mini Message demands attention, give it a "dose of drama." There's a reason why the news, reality shows and talk shows focus on the dramatic—it's memorable and creates a buzz. Blockbuster movie titles, hit TV series, smash songs or bestselling books are often good resources for inspiration, ideas and benchmarking. Remember, the key is to use a "dose," not an overdose of drama.

eXAMPLE (PRE-SMS)

Our sorority, *Alpha Beta Gamma*, is holding an event for all current and future prospective members on April 1st. Hope anyone interested can come out to this terrific event to be part of the next GR8 class!

eXAMPLE (POST-SMS)

Where do girls really wanna have fun?? Find out by joining *Alpha Beta Gamma* in our breakout new members party this April 1. Trust us, it's no April Fools'!

EXCEPTION

For Mini Messages that need to avoid, not attract, attention (fact-based or relating to issues of concern), then the "dose of drama" strategy shouldn't be used.

eXAMPLE

Our sympathies to you for your missing female chow-chow puppy, Scrappy. We at the Humane Society will notify you immediately if we hear of any similar missing dog.

RULE

11 ATTACK OF THE ACRONYMS!

Acronyms (words formed by combining the first letters of a group of words) were originally meant to save time in an era when not many acronyms existed. Today, there are acronyms galore (LOL, FYI, TMI, etc). I call this the "Attack of the Acronyms!" When the reader has to spend just as much time deciphering your acronyms than reading the other parts of the main text, you should probably scale back on those pesky letter abbreviations.

eXAMPLE (PRE-SMS)

Fyi, I just got the 911 on the DL via an IM about the newbie last nite. You'll never believe it—will blow you away! Meet @ the water cooler l8r?!

eXAMPLE (POST-SMS)

Fyi, have some interesting news. Meet later at the usual spot, usual time?

EXCEPTION

If you want "plausible deniability" relating to the content of a particular Mini Message, the Attack of the Acronyms may serve as a useful stealth device.

eXAMPLE

BM in HR is in exodus mode. Info is in the DL.

** Note*

BM=Brutal Manager

HR=Human Resources department

DL=Down Low (top secret)

RULE

CYBER-SEQUENCING 12

Have you ever received messages in multiple parts? If a victim of this, you'll know that the last message part is usually read first since it's the most recent one received. When confronted with such "multi-part" Mini Messages (texts, tweets or emails), make sure to "reverse-sequence" your messages. This way, the Mini Message receiver reads your messages in the order that you wrote them, as intended.

eXAMPLE (PRE-SMS)

[Part 3 by Sender, Part 1 for Reader]

⇒ See you then?

[Part 2 by Sender, Part 2 for Reader]

⇒ Thought that it would be really great if all of us in the club could all meet up.

[Part 1 by Sender, Part 3 for Reader]

⇒ Had a great time at last night's socializing event. You missed out.

eXAMPLE (POST-SMS)

[Part 1 by Sender, Part 3 for Reader]

⇒ Had a great time at last night's socializing event. You missed out.

[Part 2 for Reader]

⇒ Thought that it would be really great if all of us in the academic club could all meet up.

[Part 3 by Sender, Part 1 for Reader]

⇒ See you then?

[Part 1 by Sender, Part 3 for Reader]

[Part 2 for Reader and Sender]

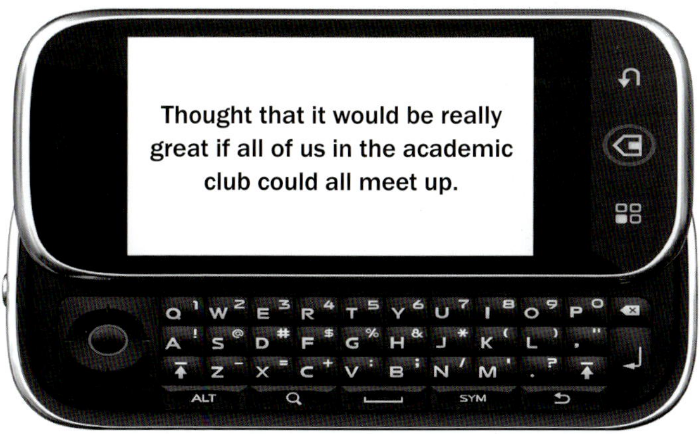

[Part 3 by Sender, Part 1 for Reader]

EXCEPTION

Generally there are few, if any, exceptions to the "Cyber-Sequencing" rule. Everyone needs to read messages in the order written to understand them. Alternatively, compress your multi-part Mini Message into one consolidated message.

eXAMPLE

Yesterday's event was great! Meet at the academic club later?

RULE

13 ONE HIT WONDERS

For single word replies, when Senders ask one specific question, it's possible to answer with a one word reply. Also, single characters such as "@" "&" and arithmetic symbols ("+" "/" ">" "1" "5" etc) are acceptable.

eXAMPLE (PRE-SMS)

[Sender] What time is the luncheon today?

[Receiver/Sender] I think 12pm is the luncheon time.

eXAMPLE (POST-SMS)

[Sender] What time is the luncheon today?

[Receiver/Sender] @12pm

[Sender]

[Receiver/Sender]

EXCEPTION

If you're trying to develop a relationship, using the "One on One" reply approach may have added language to show curiosity or interest.

eXAMPLE

[Sender] What time is the luncheon today?

[Receiver/Sender] How's it going. Glad you're going. I think 12pm is the luncheon time.

RULE 14

THE "X" FACTOR

Shortening words by using "Xs" has become increasingly commonplace. Examples are "thx," "xpress," and "xtra." I call this the "X Factor." Similarly, "Zs" are also increasingly being used. Examples are "guyz" and "plz" to name a few. If possible, spell out the term in full. It does take up more texting space. But it improves the Mini Message's style substantially.

eXAMPLE (PRE-SMS)

I xpressly told you to plz keep quiet.

eXAMPLE (POST-SMS)

I expressly told you to please keep quiet.

EXCEPTION

Purely playful or personal Mini Messages can be sprinkled with X Factors.

eXAMPLE

Come by okay....pleeezz. Xtra sugar on top!

RULE

15 ACTIVE ACTIVITY

Use the active voice when possible. This most notably includes using active verbs (and "I"). While doing this, try to convert "has been" and "have been" wording to "is" "am" or "are" statements.

eXAMPLE (PRE-SMS)

I have been giving your idea a lot of thought.

eXAMPLE (POST-SMS)

I'm giving your idea a lot of thought.

EXCEPTION

When you want to draw attention away from a certain part of your Mini Message, use the passive voice. This strategy can be used, for instance, to convey bad news.

eXAMPLE

It seems that your idea will be given a lot of thought. But so far, the feedback hasn't been spectacular.

RULE

16

NEAR MISses

Make sure that your Mini Message is void of "Near MISses"—misinterpretations, misstatements and misspellings. Most Senders just run spell check. But this doesn't catch misstated (or mistyped) words or phrases that can be misinterpreted. Checking for Near MISses will allow for peace of mind that you are "practicing safe text."

eXAMPLE (PRE-SMS)

It's a new ear with the new fall lineup.

eXAMPLE (POST-SMS)

It's a new era with the new fall lineup.

EXCEPTION

Few, if any, exceptions exist since errors are never wanted. But if done, use a combination of humor and wit to minimize the damage.

eXAMPLE

Little Mis Sunshine...woops, Little Ms. Sunshine!

RULE

17 ANGST AIKIDO

When you're a Receiver to an emotionally charged Mini Message, practice "Angst Aikido." Aikido is a Japanese martial art that uses the attacker's force back towards them. Similarly, refocus the Sender's emotional message to a more positive tone. Then resend back to the Sender.

eXAMPLE (PRE-SMS)

[Sender] Your last *Flock of Seabass* concert was a total disaster and disappointment. I want my money back now!!

[Receiver/Sender] No, that's not the way we work around here. No refunds!

eXAMPLE (POST-SMS)

[Sender] Your last *Flock of Seabass* concert was a total disaster and disappointment. I want my money back now!!

[Receiver/Sender] I understand why you may feel this way. We'll make it up to you on the next concert.

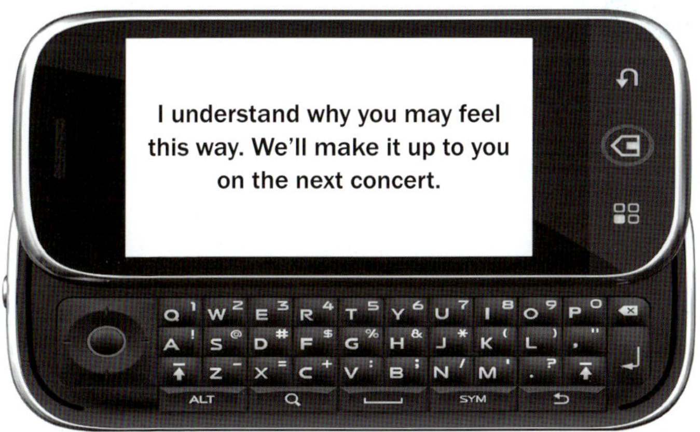

EXCEPTION

If you want to spite someone and risk ruining the relationship, then you do not need to practice Angst Aikido Attribution.

eXAMPLE

[Sender] Your last *Flock of Seabass* concert was a total disaster and disappointment. I want my money back now!!

[Receiver/Sender] Sorry you feel this way, but unfortunately, we have a strict no refund policy.

RULE 18

TEXTOSTERONE TRAPS

The Mini Message and Tech Tribe audience is large, diverse and growing everyday. This means that your Mini Message must be accommodating of this diversity. This includes avoiding "Textosterone Traps"—being unnecessarily competitive and aggressive.

eXAMPLE (PRE-SMS)

Either you take down that picture or I'll make sure your site crashes by tomorrow!

eXAMPLE (POST-SMS)

Much appreciated if you could take down that picture.

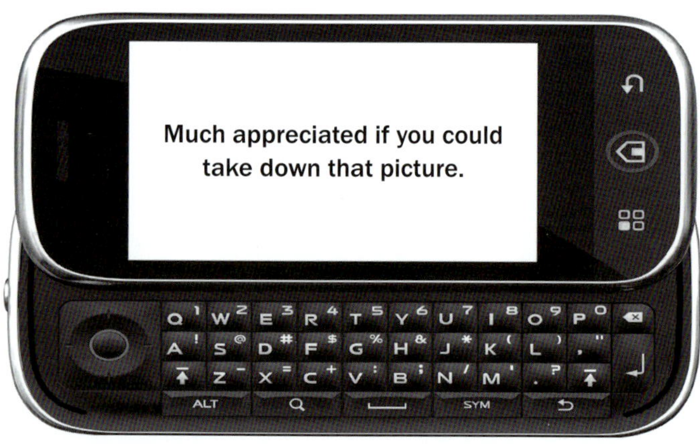

EXCEPTION

When there is no other choice but to fight fire with fire, a certain level of textosterone is understandable. Sometimes it's just "testosterone time"—for sports, bonding, negotiating, verbal jousting, etc.

eXAMPLE

That touchdown totally rocked the free world!!!

RULE

19 MICROBRAND MANAGEMENT

A "Microbrand" is a small or niche brand known to a local area or audience. Make sure that your Mini Message matches your Microbrand (corporate or personal). I call this "Microbrand Management." Otherwise you may be sending conflicting or mixed messages.

eXAMPLE (PRE-SMS)

Saturday Night feverish sale at "Like Totally" 80s retro shop this Saturday 7pm to midnite.

eXAMPLE (POST-SMS)

Manic Monday sale at "Like Totally" 80s retro shop this Monday!

EXCEPTION

If you or your firm is diversifying into a new domain, the Microbrand Management rule may not apply.

eXAMPLE

Some Kind of Wonderful sale at "Like Totally" 80s retro shop on all grunge era plaid shirts!

RULE

20 PUNS N' PROSES

Puns that use terms in an nonconventional way may be a big hit or loser. Make sure to note this risk when texting your next Mini Message.

eXAMPLE (PRE-SMS)

Trying to be "punny" by writing Puns N' Proses

eXAMPLE (POST-SMS)

Trying to be funny by writing Puns N' Proses.

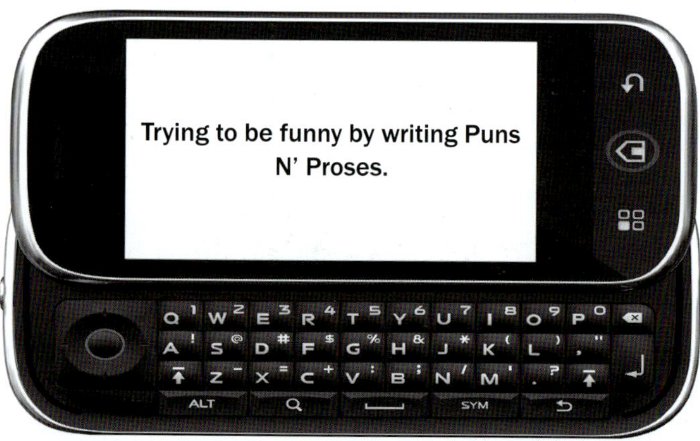

EXCEPTION

When you are writing in a serious context, avoid Puns N' Proses.

eXAMPLE

Dear Mr. Axel Tulips, sorry to hear about the last album.

THE "SCIENCE" OF SMS: 20 RULES FOR THE 2.0 ENVIRONMENT

RULE 1

EASY eNGLISH

Mini Messaging English and written English are different. Mini Messaging English is written for the Tech Tribe audience. Information must be conveyed in seconds, not days. So, it must be written with maximum efficiency. This means redefining the English language to meet this need to deliver information directly, clearly and concisely. Simplicity is elegance. I call this "Easy English" (or "Easy-E" in short).

eXAMPLE (PRE-SMS)

Indicators demonstrate that inflationary pressures will be stress-tested northward to the detriment of consumers. This will mean less disposable income in terms of GDP per capita.

eXAMPLE (POST-SMS)

Prices of goods and services may increase going forward. This means that average folks will have less money to spend.

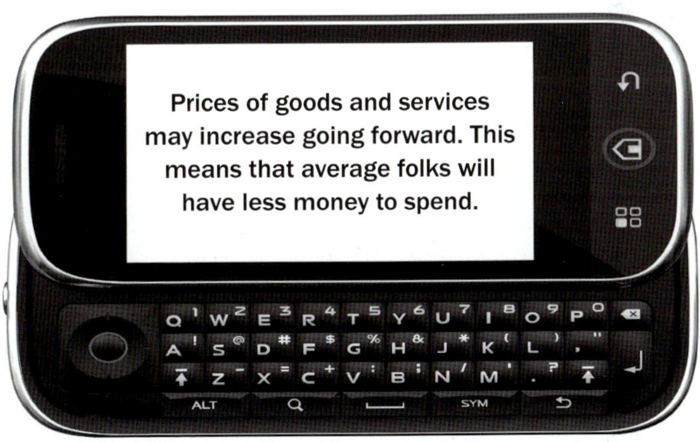

EXCEPTION

When Mini Messaging to an informed audience, Easy English may be less necessary. If so, then still apply Easy English when possible with occasional use of technical words.

eXAMPLE

Inflation—the increase in prices of goods and services—may be going up in the future. This translates into less disposable income—money left after expenses—for the average person.

RULE

2

SUBPRIME SENTENCES

All sentences are not created equal, even if sharing the same amount of texting space. Poorly written sentences—subprime sentences—should undergo "restructuring" to make them more viable and value-added. "Creditworthy" Mini Messages often begin with the subject first.

eXAMPLE (PRE-SMS)

We'd like to bring your attention to a book sale of ten percent on all mystery novels at Books R' Noble store tomorrow.

eXAMPLE (POST-SMS)

10% off all mystery novels at Books R' Noble store tomorrow!

EXCEPTION

Some "subprime sentences" may be written incorrectly on purpose. Slang, Tech Tribe lingo and quoted language taken from the media are good examples.

eXAMPLE

To boldly go where no Mini Message has gone before...

RULE

3

ZAPPING ZOMBIE WORDS

Some words take up needless space in people's Mini Messages. I call these "zombie words"—words that have physical form but serve no other purpose. Keep a watchful eye for these. And when you spot them, begin "zapping zombie words." A Mini Message beginning with "there is" or "there are" represents common zombie words that can be zapped.

eXAMPLE (PRE-SMS)

There is an urgent need for student campaign volunteers right away. For those who have interest, there will be a meeting at 9am next Tuesday at Camp Pain headquarters.

eXAMPLE (POST-SMS)

Urgent—student campaign volunteers needed! To join, meet Tuesday 9am at Camp Pain HQ.

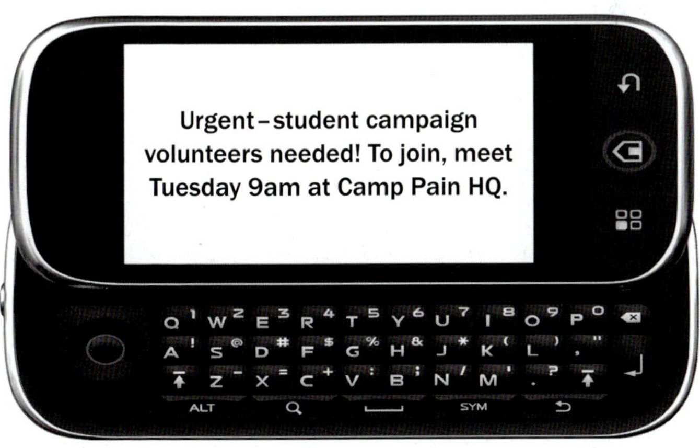

EXCEPTION

Zombie words are sometimes used to add padding or cushion to a message. One reason for this is to appear that time and effort has been used in preparing the message.

eXAMPLE

There has been considerable time and consideration put forth relating to your proposal to rezone the district. It is unfortunate that we must convey the decision to not grant this request at this time.

RULE 4

AMUSING ADJECTIVES

Adjectives exist to modify nouns or other parts of your Mini Message. They can emphasize, qualify or specify certain characteristics. So, instead of using bland "plain vanilla" adjectives, use exotic, colorful and creative adjectives. In other words, apply "Amusing Adjectives" to your Mini Messages.

eXAMPLE (PRE-SMS)

The TGIF function was a great success. And everyone who participated had a pleasant time.

eXAMPLE (POST-SMS)

The TGIF was totally fun for everyone!

EXCEPTION

Sometimes the branding and imaging of the person or place that is sending the Mini Message may not fit the "Amusing Adjectives" approach. Check first, but if some flexibility exists, try to use it.

eXAMPLE

Prepare to celebrate our firm's brand new branch opening at 2pm today.

RULE 5

VIBRANT (VALUE-ADDED) VERBS

Use "Vibrant (Value-added) Verbs" to grab attention to your Mini Message. In movie-making terms, the verb provides action to the main actor (subject). So, with any action scene, it can be fast and furious or lose its fuzz in the process.

eXAMPLE (PRE-SMS)

We were all so very happy that the movie opening gala was a grand success.

eXAMPLE (POST-SMS)

We were elated that the movie opening gala was a huge success.

EXCEPTION

Vibrant value-added verbs could reflect over-exuberance. If you believe a more measured approach is better, then use traditional "plain vanilla" verbs.

eXAMPLE

We weren't crushed, but disappointed to find out we couldn't score tickets for the Duran Duran tribute band concert.

RULE 6

NOMINALIZATIONS OF NOMINAL VALUE

Avoid using nominalizations—the process of converting certain words into non-verbs (e.g., "nominal" is an adjective and "nominalization" is a nominalization). The reason is that nominalizations take up valuable texting space. Instead base verbs serve the same function, take up less space and are more reader-friendly. This is why they are "nominalizations of nominal value."

eXAMPLE (PRE-SMS)

We felt great satisfaction in our purchase of our "Ice, Ice Baby" snowboard for our new toddler.

eXAMPLE (POST-SMS)

We were extremely satisfied after buying our toddler's "Ice, Ice Baby" snowboard.

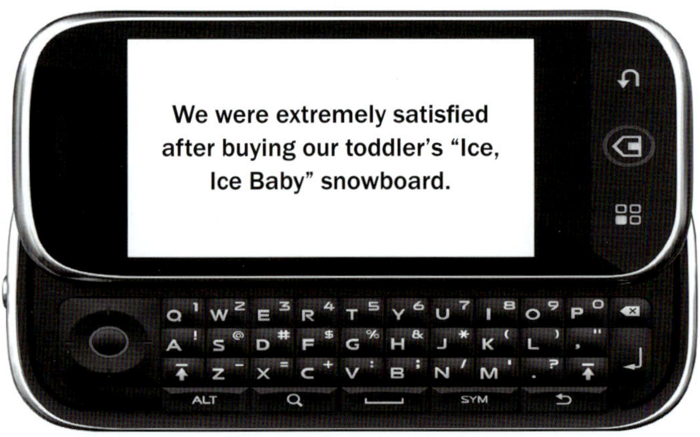

EXCEPTION

Policies or clear precedents may be better served as nominalizations. So, if this is the case, the "nominalizations of nominal value" need not apply.

eXAMPLE

Emancipation Proclamation (or "Satisfaction Guaranteed")

RULE

7 PREPOSITIONAL PREPPIES

Some Mini Messagers have a habit that's hard to kick—using prepositional phrases in their sentences. I call these writers "prepositional preppies." This is because prepositional phrases—words like "of" "in" and "above"—are mostly for appearances backed by little or no substance. So, it's important to avoid these prepositional phrase pitfalls.

eXAMPLE (PRE-SMS)

Welcome Class of 2010 to our new Department of Pseudo Sciences!

eXAMPLE (POST-SMS)

Welcome Class of 2010 to our new Pseudo Sciences Department.

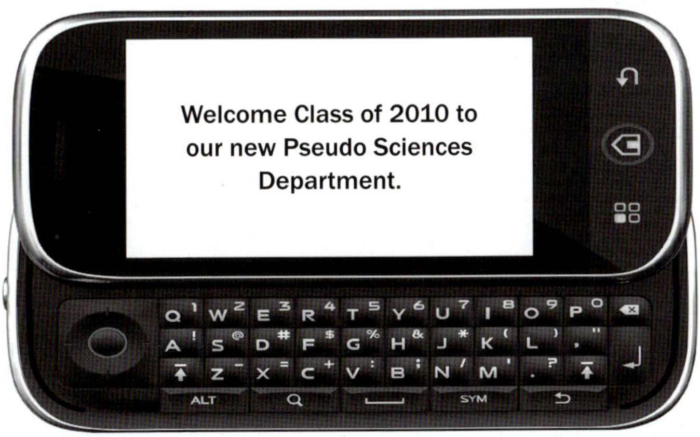

EXCEPTION

Titles and positions can have prepositional phrases to reflect historical essence, status and rank. If you are in this situation, you can keep "prepositional preppies" in place.

eXAMPLE

Professor of Pseudo Sciences (rather than "Pseudo Sciences Professor")

RULE 8

JEDI JARGON

The Jedi was an elite class of warriors portrayed in the *Star Wars* movie trilogies. When talking with each other, the Jedi would often speak using Jedispeak—words only decipherable by other Jedi. But unlike Jedi, most Mini Messagers want to reach a broad audience of all types, backgrounds and profiles. So, using insider language, terms and jargon—what I call "Jedi Jargon"—is not in your best interest and should be avoided.

eXAMPLE (PRE-SMS)

Police reported a GTA by a possible 5150 individual.

eXAMPLE (POST-SMS)

Police reported a stolen car incident by a person who may be crazy or uncontrollable.

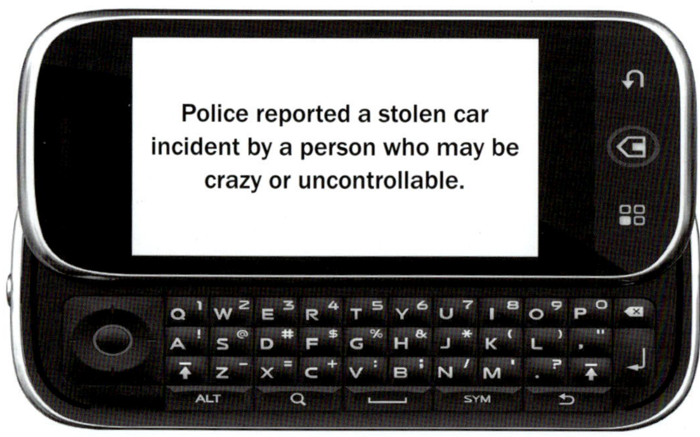

EXCEPTION

When speaking to other Jedi or using Jedi Jargon that may be known by the general public, then Jedi Jargon can be used with others outside the Jedi Council.

eXAMPLE

Our ETA should be around 9pm tonight.

RULE

9

CAPPING CAPS

Writing in all caps gets attention. But it may be misconstrued to mean that the Sender is angry or upset. If you use all caps, then do so at your peril. Otherwise, it's best to put a cap on your caps—what I call "capping caps." Also, generally begin your sentences with caps.

eXAMPLE (PRE-SMS)

HEY GUYS, WHAT'S THE PLAN FOR DINNER TO-NIGHT??

eXAMPLE (POST-SMS)

Hey Guys. What's the plan for DINNER tonight??

EXCEPTION

In times of emergency or lack of time, use all caps to get first priority attention from the Reader.

eXAMPLE

GUYS, I NEED FOOD NOW! WHO'S UP FOR DIN-NER?!

RULE 10

LEGALLY BLAND

If any of you have had to read any legal instrument, you'll know that legal English is not only technical, but sometimes boring and bland. If you write like this, then you're being "Legally Bland." This is usually not a compliment. And try to avoid the use of unnecessary legalese-type language. Often "thereto," "aforementioned," and "with respect to" are good indicators of a Mini Message entering the "Legally Bland zone."

eXAMPLE (PRE-SMS)

With respect to where to conduct our next meeting, we believe the venues listed herein should suffice.

eXAMPLE (POST-SMS)

We believe any of the locations below should be fine for our next meeting.

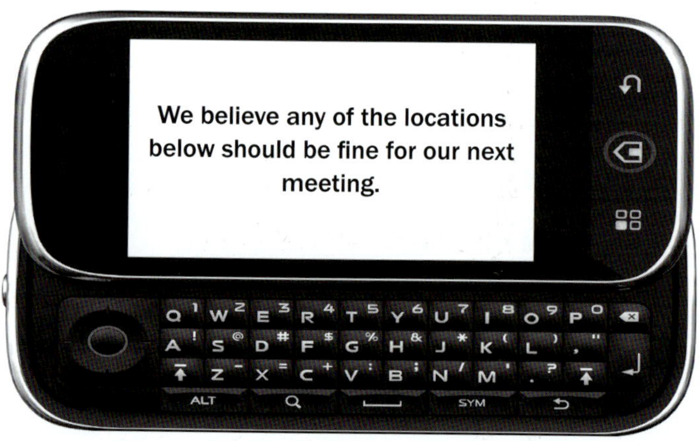

EXCEPTION

If you want to baffle and bedazzle using the smoke and mirrors of the Legally Bland zone (or if you actually are in the legal profession), then being Legally Bland is not a violation of good Mini Messaging.

eXAMPLE

With respect to the issues discussed, we believe that the related action items therein, such as an on-campus coop and an organic garden, with the former taking precedence over the latter, may be furthered after securing the requisite budget.

RULE 11

YUP, WE CAN!?

"Yup" is usually used as an informal "yes." And it is no problem for informal occasions. But imagine if Barack Obama's presidential campaign motto was "Yup, We Can!" (rather than "Yes, We Can!")? You can probably feel the difference. Using "yes" has an aura to it that "yup" simply can not match for more formal occasions. So, based on the situation, using "yes" than "yup" will exude trust in you, your "microbrand" or whatever organization you represent.

eXAMPLE (PRE-SMS)

Yup, We Can!

eXAMPLE (POST-SMS)

Yes, We Can!

EXCEPTION

When speaking with your "inner circle" of close acquaintances, using "yup" (or "yep") can also work.

eXAMPLE

Yup, just finished the final exam. Or more like, the final exam finished me!

RULE 12

TOXIC TERMS

Certain terms are toxic. These “toxic terms” are often linked to sensitive issues (politics, religion, race, gender, etc) and should be avoided

eXAMPLE (PRE-SMS)

Pacman

eXAMPLE (POST-SMS)

Pacperson

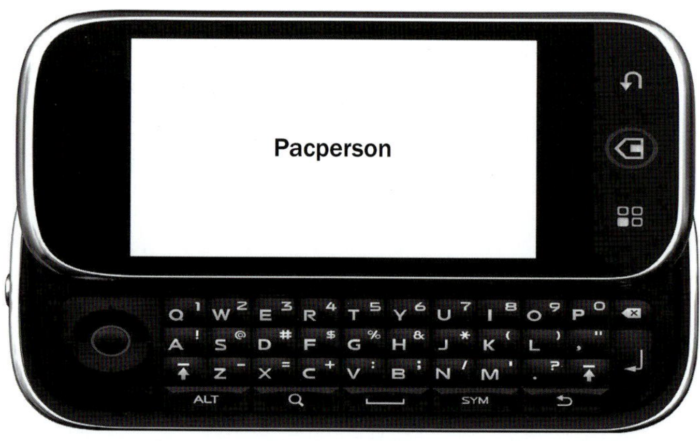

EXCEPTION

If you want to elicit controversy, use Toxic Terms. But do so at your peril.

eXAMPLE

All men are stupid. All women are crazy. (the remaining part of this adage is "....and all women are crazy because all men are stupid.")

RULE

13 QWERTY OR QUIRKY

Two types of Mini Messaging writing styles exist. First, “QWERTY” style writing (reflecting the standard keyboard) is the traditional writing approach where words are used in standard form and not shortened. Second, the “QUIRKY” writing style often used in the Web 2.0 world uses shortened words, acronyms and e-slang. Generally, for business purposes, use the QWERTY approach. It is more clear and professional. For social purposes, apply a 80/20 approach—80% QWERTY and 20% QUIRKY.

eXAMPLE (PRE-SMS)

Sending txt msg 4ur 411, LOL :)

eXAMPLE (POST-SMS)

Text message being sent as an fyi. Thanks.

** Note*

fyi=for your information

EXCEPTION

Apply the "when in Twitter, do as the Tweeters do" mantra. In other words, blend in with local customs and practices to use the QUIRKY writing style.

eXAMPLE

Loved your last Tweet. Can you retweet?

RULE 14

VERSES VS. VERSUS

Your Mini Message's tone can either be written in "verses" or "versus." "Verses" are written in either a neutral or positive tone. "Versus" are written in either a confrontational, combative or otherwise negative tone (sometimes unintentionally). Keep high "quality control" for your Mini Message by tweaking your Mini Message wording to be written in "verses" not "versus."

eXAMPLE (PRE-SMS)

What were you thinking with that last comment??!!

eXAMPLE (POST-SMS)

Your last comment was mildly shocking.

EXCEPTION

If you firmly believe an aggressive tone is needed (negotiations, unreasonable Receiver, etc), then use a moderate amount of "versus" tone in your Mini Message.

eXAMPLE

Your last comment was clearly unreasonable. I recommend you retract it immediately.

RULE 15

LATIN LOVERS

With "Latin Lovers" (Senders who enjoy using Latin, French, Italics and non-English words), try to use its English equivalent to maximize readership. Else, opt not to use them.

eXAMPLE (PRE-SMS)

Why are you raising this *ex post facto*?

eXAMPLE (POST-SMS)

Why are you raising this after the fact?

EXCEPTION

When Mini Messaging with other Latin Lovers, then using Latin Lovers may be a more efficient mode of communication. Some foreign terms may also have been incorporated fully into the English language. If so, then being a "Latin Lover" is perfectly acceptable.

eXAMPLE

Fellow economists, the economy should grow by 1.5% next fiscal year, ceteris peribus. If so, "asta la vista, baby"—Governor Terminator.

* *Note*

ceteris peribus=all things being equal

asta la vista=see you later

RULE 16

O'BROTHER (WHERE ART THOU)

Generally avoid using terms of friendship and familiarity when unsubstantiated. Terms like "brother" "bro" "dude" "sister" "man" and so on may be testing a relationship that does not need to be tested.

eXAMPLE (PRE-SMS)

Dude, where's my car?!

eXAMPLE (POST-SMS)

Where's my car?!

EXCEPTION

If certain terms of friendship and familiarity are the accepted norm, then exercise your freedom and best judgment as to using the "O'Brother" rule.

eXAMPLE

Man, that's what I call a slam dunk!

RULE 17

ALLITERATION ALLURE

An "alliteration" is a series of words each beginning with the same first letter. "Alliteration Allure" is one example. Use Alliteration Allure to draw interest and curiosity. The content may be the same. But the packaging is much more appealing.

eXAMPLE (PRE-SMS)

Twins from the Thomson family go on tour.

eXAMPLE (POST-SMS)

Thomson Twins Tour.

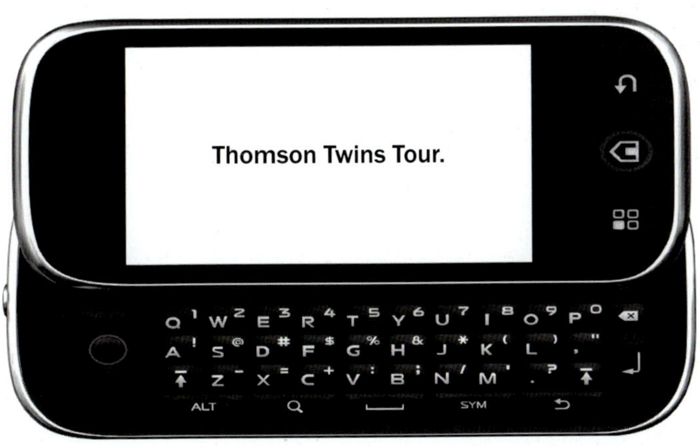

EXCEPTION

Poetic alliterations are not for everyone. If you believe that the direct approach will be more effective (compared to a memorable catchphrase), then using Alliteration Allure may not always be needed.

eXAMPLE

Tour for the Thomson Twins.

RULE 18

JUST SAY NO TO S-V-O! (SUBJECT-VERB-OBJECT)

A sound sentence often follows the S-V-O structure (Subject-Verb-Object). In our "2.0 world," however, texting space represents coveted real estate. So, many sentences can be shortened by following the Verb-Object structure (without the Subject).

eXAMPLE (PRE-SMS)

I really enjoyed the lecture yesterday.

eXAMPLE (POST-SMS)

Really enjoyed yesterday's lecture.

EXCEPTION

If you want to place emphasis on the subject, then use the S-V-O sentence structure approach.

eXAMPLE

The Tofu Fighters will be giving a live performance tonight.

RULE

19 APPLIED PHDs (PUNCTUATIONS, HYPHENS AND DOTS)

Mini Messagers should normally take an "Applied PHD" approach (using Punctuations, Hyphens and Dots). Using the Applied PHD approach shows attention to detail and exactness. If your Mini Messages appear decent on paper, they most likely will be decent without paper (I call this the "Pretty in Ink" test).

eXAMPLE (PRE-SMS)

breaking news, dawn johnson wears socks with shoes—stay tuned

eXAMPLE (POST-SMS)

Breaking news—Dawn Johnson wears socks with shoes. Stay tuned for more details!

EXCEPTION

Not using Applied PHDs can reflect a sense of urgency. For Senders who are in broadcasting or other fields covering breaking news or sudden events, Applied PHDs can be be used less frequently.

eXAMPLE

Breaking news...Dawn Johnson wears socks!

"TRIPLE A" PAPER (ATTACHMENTS, ADDENDUMS AND APPENDICES)

RULE 20

Once in a while, you will get Mini Messages with Attachments, Addendums and Appendices. I call these "Triple A" Paper. When you send this type of Mini Message, make a quick reference to the fact that Triple A Paper is attached. The Mini Message should not replicate any Triple A Paper content to avoid being redundant.

eXAMPLE (PRE-SMS)

I am an applicant for your DJ position. Attached is my resume. I graduated from DJ Technical School and have DJ'd for local clubs for the past 2 years. Thank you very much. DJ Dan

eXAMPLE (POST-SMS)

I am an applicant for your DJ position. Attached is my CV. Thank you and look forward to speaking with you soon. DJ Dan

EXCEPTION

If you want to highlight 1 to 2 aspects of Triple A Paper attachments, then do so in a brief line.

eXAMPLE

I am applying for your DJ position. I was rated the best DJ by *Don't Hang the DJ* magazine, graduated top in my class at DJ Technical School and have vast DJing experience. Can't wait to hear from you soon!
DJ Dan

(mini) AUTHOR PROFILE

Jasper Kim

Jasper Kim is Department Chair, Graduate School of International Studies, Ewha Womans University. He is a U.S.-licensed lawyer, former investment banker and Founder of Ohmydocs.com (an open writing website for students). He has been featured in the *BBC Worldwide TV/Radio*, *The Wall Street Journal*, *New York Times*, *Bloomberg News*, *Korea Herald*, and other media sources.